W9-AAT-316

Spiders

Laura K. Murray

CREATIVE EDUCATION • CREATIVE PAPERBACKS

Published by Creative Education and Creative Paperbacks
P.O. Box 227, Mankato, Minnesota 56002
Creative Education and Creative Paperbacks
are imprints of The Creative Company
www.thecreativecompany.us

Design by Ellen Huber
Production by Travis Green
Art direction by Rita Marshall
Printed in Malaysia

Photographs by Alamy (Antje Schulte-Spiders and Co.), Corbis
(Kjell Sandved/Visuals Unlimited, Damon Wilder), Dreamstime
(Alessandrozocc, Mario Čehulić, Designpicssub, Christian
Fernandez, Stephanie Hayes, Imarly, Isselee, Johnbell, Cathy
Keifer, Olga Khoroshunova, Paul Looyen), iStockphoto
(Blair_witch, johnaudrey, naturephotographer, spxChrome),
Shutterstock (Eric Isselee, Sebastian Janicki, Kletr), Science
Source (Scott Linstead)

Copyright © 2016 Creative Education, Creative Paperbacks
International copyright reserved in all countries.
No part of this book may be reproduced in any form
without written permission from the publisher.

Library of Congress Cataloging-in-Publication Data
Murray, Laura K.
Spiders / Laura K. Murray.
p. cm. — (Seedlings)
Includes bibliographical references and index.
Summary: A kindergarten-level introduction to spiders,
covering their growth process, behaviors, the places they call
home, and such defining features as their legs.
ISBN 978-1-60818-584-9 (hardcover)
ISBN 978-1-62832-189-0 (pbk)
1. Spiders—Juvenile literature. I. Title.

QL458.4.M877 2015
592'.3—dc23   2014034722

CCSS: RI.K.1, 2, 3, 4, 5, 6, 7;
RI.1.1, 2, 3, 4, 5, 6, 7; RF.K.1, 3; RF.1.1

First Edition HC 9 8 7 6 5 4 3 2 1
First Edition PBK 9 8 7 6 5 4 3 2 1

TABLE OF CONTENTS

Hello, spiders!

Spiders are animals that make silk.

They like dark places. They live in trees and under rocks. They live in houses, too!

Spiders have
eight legs. They
use body parts
called spinnerets
to make silk.

Most spiders have eight eyes. Some spiders have lots of hair!

Big, hairy spiders
can eat frogs or mice.
Other spiders eat bugs.

They have
fangs for biting.

A baby spider comes out of an egg. It grows bigger. Then it sheds its skin.

Many spiders
make sticky webs.

They catch food.
Then they rest.

Goodbye, spiders!

Picture a Spider

fangs

spinnerets

head

eye

legs

pedipalps

hair

abdomen

Words to Know

fangs: sharp mouthparts

sheds: gets rid of

silk: soft threads

webs: nets of silk

Read More

Bodden, Valerie. *Spiders.*
Mankato, Minn.: Creative Education, 2011.

Johnson, Jinny. *What's It Like to Be a Spider?*
Mankato, Minn.: Amicus, 2012.

Websites

DLTK's Spider Craft Projects
http://www.dltk-kids.com/crafts/insects/crafts-spiders.htm
Click on a fun spider craft. Or print out a coloring page.

Spider Puzzles
http://kids.nationalgeographic.com/kids/games
/puzzlesquizzes/spiders-puzzler/
Put together puzzles of spiders!

Note: Every effort has been made to ensure that the websites listed above are suitable for children, that they have educational value, and that they contain no inappropriate material. However, because of the nature of the Internet, it is impossible to guarantee that these sites will remain active indefinitely or that their contents will not be altered.

Index

OCEAN COUNTY LIBRARY

3 3500 0055 50355

JACKSON TOWNSHIP BRANCH

Ocean County Library
2 Jackson Drive
Jackson, NJ 08527

2/16